Views & Reminiscences of Old Greenock.

Published by Magic Torch

Published by Magic Torch

ISBN 0-9539065-1-5

Printed by Govan Litho

Originally published April 1891

This edition first published September 2001

Typeset by Magic Torch
with assistance from
Becky Mitchell
Hayley Bristow

Thanks to Inverclyde Community Development Trust

All profits from the sale of this book will be donated to Ardgowan Hospice

Magic Torch, The Westburn Centre, 175 Dalrymple Street, Greenock, Scotland, PA15 1JZ
email : magictorchgroup@hotmail.com

"There are those who see in the removal of old fabrics nothing but the displacement of so much material;

but there are others more highly organised, whose quick sympathies and poetic imaginations enable them to re-people the vacant places with the human forms that dwelt therein.

Such, sensitively alive to the lessons of the historical, surround themselves with the associations of the long ago, which emphasise the transitoriness of affairs.."

Williamson 1891

Views on Views

110 years ago, the original publishers of *Views And Reminiscences* set out to produce a volume which would "be regarded by Greenockians as a treasured window, opening out on scenes and glimpses of the fading history and local past." More than anything they wanted people to take an interest in their towns past, to show them what it once looked like, to have them read about how things used to be. And it was not just for the people of the time that they intended this, but also for future generations, so that things might not be forgotten or lost. What a tragedy then that the book itself seemed to slip through the gaps somewhere along the way, lost to rigours of time.

Today only a handful of original copies remain, mostly in libraries or private collections, where for decades, these pieces of our history, have sat gathering dust, shut away from those for whom they were intended, forgotten and unappreciated. Hardly what Mr Downie and Mr Williamson, or any authors for that matter, would have intended for their book.

But now, over 100 years later, the dust has been cleared from this "window on the past" and these Views and Reminiscences are once again in the hands of the people they were meant for. You.

Books are meant to be enjoyed.

We hope you enjoy this one.

Magic Torch
July 2001

Views and Reminiscences of Old Greenock

The publishers of "Views and Reminiscences Of Old Greenock" in issuing a volume that aims at recalling portions of the town that have passed away, have reason to believe that they are appealing to a widespread feeling of local patriotism that will secure an adequate appreciation of the work. They are, indeed, pleased to state that as regards its purport such appreciation is already assured, as leading citizens who have been consulted have warmly signified approval. While, however, grateful that the general idea of the undertaking is one that meets with commendation, they are concious that everything depends upon execution; and that success falls to be determined by the qualities of the work itself. On this point they have simply to add that they have availed themselves of the best means at their disposal to produce a memorial volume that would not only meet with acceptance now, but be regarded by Greenockians to come as a treasured window, opening out on scenes and glimpses of the local past. The raison d'etre of the enterprise lies in the numerous removals consequent on town improvements.

Few places in Scotland have undergone such a radical transformation as has Greenock in recent years. With an ear attuned to the pleadings of social and sanitary reform, she has, earlier than most towns, widened her streets, renewed her buildings, and arrayed herself in an attire of cleanliness that is in pleasing contrast with her insanitary past. In an economic sense the cost has been considerable, but the community have their reward in the knowledge that the town which was once notorious for its high death-rate is now recognised as one of the healthiest in the kingdom. If, however, Greenock can be congratulated on her improved sanitary and architectural condition, the change has not been effected without some little shock to public feeling caused by the removal of familiar and time-honoured structures which have served the purpose of many generations. It is true that many of these consisted of old "rookeries" or delapidated tenements that had become a nuisance to modern civilisation;but it cannot be forgotten that in earlier times some of them were the honoured abodes of prominent citizens, and, as such, were not without interest to the lovers of the antique.

Of the demolished buildings , some were object lessons in human progress, while others were invaluable as centres of gracious thoughts and tender memories. Among those showing the evolutionary links connecting the present with the past, were the old Greenock Mansion House, the old Greenock Prison, and the old Town Offices, while deeper feeling was stirred by such priceless possessions as the house in William Street where James Watt was born, and that in Charles Street in which Mary of the "To Mary In Heaven" breathed her last. The object of the present work is to rescue, as far as possible, such old Greenock landmarks from oblivion; to set, as it were, the once familiar places on the canvas, to recall notable persons and events, and, generally speaking, to give the citizen of to-day, who knows Greenock as it is, some idea of Greenock as it was.

It is not forgotten that Greenock has her historians in Mr Daniel Weir, Mr Dugald Campbell, and Mr George Williamson; but it may be emphasised that whereas their work consists almost entirely of letterpress, the publishers of the present volume rely more upon the illuminating power of art. The illustrations, which have been carefuly lithographed in the publishers premises are from drawings by Mr P Downie, artist, Paisley, formely of Greenock, and from photographs and other pictures. For the letterpress, the publishers are indebted to Mr A Williamson, late of Greenock, and now of Edinburgh, who has, with much care, gathered and put in literary form the available information bearing on the various pictures. "Views and Reminiscences of Old Greenock," though perhaps finding little favour with the cold, calculating intellect, will appeal to all who take a delight in the play of fancy, and love to linger in the realms of the retrospective "It is curious" says an eminent living writer "that the saddest and most touching of human thoughts, when we run it up to its simplest form, if of so lonely a thing as a material object, exisiting in a certain space and then removed from that space to another. That is the essential idea of 'Gone.'" It is also this idea of "Gone" that has produced the present work; and while a pensive atmosphere may more or less intrude itself throughout its pages, they are certain to call forth pleasurable moods, in which subtle links of relationship between old and the new reveal themselves, suggesting the thoughts that mellow the outlook, and touching the memory to gentler and more tolerant issues. To-day, in some quarters, sentiment is regarded somewhat askance, but most assuredly of this commodity the busy struggling world has not overmuch.

"History storms on with siege and battle and political crisis, but poety runs alongside, supplementing history, smoothing its austerities, and filling up its chasms and interstices with music."

That "Views and Reminiscences of Old Greenock" with its fading history and vanishing past, may also distil somewhat of the music of humanity, and yield delight, is the ardent wish of the publishers.

Greenock, April, 1891

I
Greenock From The Clyde

The contrast between the Greenock of 1825 and that of today is marked indeed. Since 1801 it has advanced from a place of comparative unimportance to a town and seaport of no small significance. The lapse of time is striking, but no less so than the advancements which have taken place within it. For example, in 1811, Greenock was still without gas, an advantage first enjoyed by the citizens seventeen years later. The town was well served for many years by the original works, situated in the Glebe; but the growth of the community and its progress in sanitation called for the new and extensive works at Inchgreen, which were opened in 1873. The harbour accommodation at Greenock in 1811 was exceedingly limited as compared with the splendid shipping facilities offered by the port today. Greenock may be said to have possessed no harbour works until 1710, when, as the result of the enterprise of the then inhabitants, the East and West harbours, forming an amphitheatre inclosing the Mid Quay at the base, had sprung into existence. The citizens of the time had bound themselves to an assessment of one shilling and fourpence on every sack of malt brewed into ale within the limits of the town, the revenue therefrom to the building and equipping of harbours. In 1792 the whole harbour dues amounted to just a little over £800, a mere bagatelle as compared to the harbour revenues of today.

The original harbour works as completed in 1710, at a cost of something under £6000, though appearing as insignificant to the citizen of today, were considered formidable at the time, and were recognised as the greatest of the kind in Scotland. Since then the Harbour accommodation and the trade of the port have developed hand in hand: and the extent of this progress may be read in the following statements. What is known as the New Graving Dock was completed in 1824 at a cost of £20,000; the Victoria Harbour was opened in 1850; the Albert Harbour was ready for traffic in 1867; the Garvel Graving Dock was finished in 1873; and the first vessel was floated into the magnificent James Watt Dock on the 5th August 1886. Our staple industries of shipbuilding and sugar refining had early established themselves in Greenock. Weir, writing in 1829 says "Shipbuilding from an early period has been carried on with great success, but previous to the breaking out of the American war, almost all the vessels belonging to the Clyde were built in America." The tables have now been completely turned on the Americans, whose economic policy has almost silenced their shipbuilding industry; while that of the various marine centres throughout the United Kingdom goes forward by leaps and bounds.

The first sugar house in Greenock was built in 1765; and in 1829 there were no fewer than seven refineries at work. The out-turn, however, from the refineries at that time, with their slow going methods, was insignificant as compared with that of today. In 1889 the quantity of sugar turned out from our Greenock Refineries was 240,000 tons. In the earlier years of the century, Greenock was in possession of industries which have perished. These included straw-hat making, the manufacture of silk and felt hats, with bottle and flint glass works and others. These works afforded considerable employment and there removal in to be regretted. The town has had in recent years its commercial ups and downs; but, considering its unrivalled situation, its magnificent harbours, its numerous railway connections and its splendid water supplies, there is every reason to believe that an early future will see it crowned with increasing prosperity.

Greenock from the Clyde

II
Toll Bar and Cappielow Inn ; Port Glasgow Road

Toll-Bars in combination with inns or public houses have not been infrequent in Scotland. The Toll-Bar has perished, but the inn remains to minister the wants of the wayfarer. The accompanying picture brings before us Cappielow Inn and Toll-Bar, on the Port Glasgow Road. This once famous place of public resort, which has served its day, was for many a year familiar as a milestone to the passer-by.

There is associated with Cappielow, which was a halfway house or resting place between the two ports, a story not unworthy of being recorded. The incident happened very long ago, but it has the merit of being well founded. In the earlier years of the century, and at midnight, fire broke out in a public work situated in Cartsdyke; and as the fire-extinguishing apparatus of the Port Glasgow Corporation was believed to be superior to that of Greenock, it was resolved at all hazards that it should be procured for the occasion. Everything depended on promptitude of action, and thereupon Mr Donald McNicol, a well-known Greenock citizen of the time, sprung upon horseback and proceeding at galloping pace, reached the Cappielow Toll-Bar at almost a bound. Finding the way barred, he summoned old Dumbreck, the toll-keeper of the day, to open the gates; but not meeting with an immediate response, he spurred his horse, and clearing the barriers swiftly found himself and his message in the Port. The speed at which McNicol made the journey may be realised when it is stated that on returning and clearing the Toll-Bar as before, old Dumbreck was seen peeping out and rubbing his eyes as if emerging from sleep, and evidently under the impression that he was promptly answering the summons of McNicol to open the gates.

Happily in our day the possession of efficient fire brigades and telephones obviates the necessity of such desperate adventures.

Toll Bar and Cappielow Inn

11

III
Garvel Park House and Grounds

This picture represents, though not exactly in its present form, a section of Eastern Greenock which of late has become prominent through the construction of the magnificent James Watt Dock. The mansion house on Garvel Park estate is still left standing, though robbed of its former glory and surroundings. It is no longer a family residence, having become, in common with the grounds themselves, a victim to the trading and commercial requirements of the time.

Garvel Park Mansion House was built by Bailie Gammell, the prosperous Greenock merchant and banker, who had the honour of being one of the founders of the Greenock Bank. On leaving Greenock, this gentleman retired to the north of Scotland, where he acquired extensive landed estates, which are still in the possession of his descendants. Garvel Park estate was acquired in 1832 from Mr Gammell's trustees, by Mr John Scott, of Hawkhill, father of Mr Charles Cunningham Scott, the world renowned shipbuilder. It was occupied and brought into the condition represented in the picture, by Mr Robert Sinclair, son-in-law of Mr John Scott, of Hawkhill, who made it hisA residence. Mr Sinclair was the managing partner of the firm of Scott, Sinclair & Co., of the Greenock Foundry Company, the business of which is carried on by the descendants of the original founders, on a greatly extended scale. In 1855, after the death of Sinclair, Garvel Park estate passed to her brother, Mr Charles Cunningham Scott, then of Hawkhill, the father of the present Messrs. John and Robert Sinclair Scott. In 1868 it became the property of the Greenock Harbour Trust, which had acquired it in order to meet the growing shipping wants of the port.

The new graving dock was constructed some few years afterwards; and more recently there has sprung into being the James Watt Dock, which, while unfortunately not yet too well utilised, is recognised by merchants and ship owners as one of the very finest in the kingdom.

Garvel Park House and Grounds

IV
The Cartsburn Mansion House

The accompanying illustration represents the Mansion House of the lands of the Cartsburn as it existed before the industrial growth of Eastern Greenock had encroached on the policies and then marred the amenity of the place as a family residence.

Cartsburn has a very old history, the earlier stages of which it is now somewhat difficult to trace. In or about the middle of the seventeenth century, Thomas Crawfurd obtained a Crown charter, whereby the lands of Cartsburn represented as a plain, old fashioned structure. It is understood to have been built towards the end of the seventeenth century, when it was no longer necessary that the house of the gentry should be formed as places of defence.

Cartsburn House is now utilised for other purposes , and part of the old building may still be seen off Ingleston Road, over the Cartsburn.

The Cartsburn Mansion House

V
The Old Mansion-House

No Greenockian will fail to recognise in this picture the once familiar features of the old Greenock Mansion-House, which was removed in 1886 by the Caledonian Railway Company when constructing their branch line to Gourock. Greenock has but little to engage the attention of the antiquary; and, in the disappearance of the Mansion-House, it has lost a building which spoke to it through the voice of the centuries. Great regret was felt at this destruction, and no wonder, for it may be said to have presided over the birth, and witnessed the development of the town. To delineate the history of the Mansion-House would be not only to narrate the rise and progress of Greenock, but to trace the development of civilisation.

The old House, with its attractive architectural features and its altogether quaint appearance, is understood to have weathered the storms for four centuries. It is impossible to fix the exact date of its erection, but the main portion of the building, to which additions had been made from time to time, is believed to have existed as far back as the fourteenth century. Up to the period of its demolition it was still possible , with a little trouble, to decipher here and there dates impressed on stones connected with the buildings. In the Mansion-House itself the dates 1635 and 1674 were to be traced, while in connection with the draw-well of the ancient Manorial House, so familiar to Wellpark visitors, might have been seen the figures 1629. For generations the Mansion-House was the residence of Sir Michael Robert Shaw Stewart's ancestors. In the olden time, ere the mere fishing village had developed into modern Greenock with its sugar and shipbuilding industries, there was quietness instead of bustle, and in those days the policies of the Mansion-House were both large and extensive. Eastwards and Westwards they stretched in luxuriant plantations, running southwards to Whinhill and Northwards to the shores of the Firth.

The prospect from the Mansion-House was one of the finest. It stood upon a fine rising ground above the Assembly Rooms, and commanded a most extensive view of the town. The situation, before it was encroached upon by the erection of new buildings rendered necessary by the growth of the town, must have been one of delightful retirement and beauty. A writer in a Glasgow journal, commenting on the demolition of the old Mansion-House says; "While it remained the abode of the Schaws, it was a palatial house. The race was generous race, kindly and patriotic, entertaining the Duke of Argyll at one time, at another raising troops for the King, building harbours for the people and representing them in Parliament."

It is now fully a hundred years since the Mansion-House ceased to be the family residence. It was at that time taken possession of by the officials who managed the Greenock estates, the then Lord of the Manor betaking himself to Ardgowan, now the seat of Sir Michael Robert Shaw Stewart. A history of great importance, though unfortunately now for the most part lost in the mists of antiquity, gathers around the old Greenock Mansion-House. Various stories have been handed down, and of those the most popular is, that during the long and sanguinary Napoleonic wars, some French prisoners had been taken from the Tail-of-the-bank, and confined in a gloomy looking cell in the Mansion-House. It may be also interesting to note that the latest addition to the house took place about 1740, and that the builder was James Watt, the father of the great engineer, whose achievements have made Greenock famous the wide world o'er. The old Mansion-House marked the passage from the old to the new; and as an ancient landmark, clothed with old associations and stirring memories, was more eloquent than the pen of the historian, in showing us the evolutionary steps from the rude and barbarous to the more refined stages of today. The exigencies of the iron horse are at war with the tastes of the poet and the antiquary, but it is to be regretted that there was not sufficient spirit in Greenock to preserve for historical purposes the invaluable landmark of the old Greenock Mansion-House.

The Old Mansion House

VI
The East Quay Lane

A glance at this picture shows that it speaks to young and old Greenockians alike. It is at once suggestive of the extremely old and the very recent. What was so long known as the East Quay Lane has perished at the hands of the Improvement Trust, whose enlightened but costly operations, largely directed by Dr. Wallace, have greatly modernised the centre of the town, and improved the health of the community. In place of the narrow unsanitary passage through which travellers made their way from Cathcart Street Station to Customhouse Quay, we have now a spacious thoroughfare opening towards the river, a marked improvement which not only facilitates public convenience, but confers a new dignity on that quarter of the town. This fine new avenue, connecting Cathcart Street with the old Steamboat Quay, has fittingly been named Brymner Street, in recognition of the memorable services rendered by the late Bailie Graham Brymner in his capacity as a prominent member of the Improvement Trust. The old Caledonian Station, with which we had been familiar for almost half a century, has also been removed, to make way for the transformation rendered necessary by the formation of the Gourock Railway.

It seems but only yesterday since these landmarks disappeared, but sure enough they have now, with their chequered history, faded away into the dreamland of old Greenock. A becoming reverence for the old is not incompatible with a due appreciation of the new; and there must be few Greenockians who do not rejoice that the East Quay lane has given way to a more spacious outlet to that river. Its existence was a most ungracious advertisement for Greenock; and the thousands of strangers passing through it from year to year, on their way to the coast, must have carried away with them to all quarters of the world unsavoury and unlovely impressions of the town and the port. It was suggested some twenty five years ago, that in order to promote the comfort and convenience of the passengers, the old lane should be roofed over, and negotiations for this purpose were entered into between the Corporation and the Railway Company. The attempt however proved fruitless, and public interest in the question subsided on the opening of the Greenock and Ayrshire Line in 1869, with its fine new outlet to the coast from Princes Pier. The passenger traffic from Princes Pier, which for many years was flourishing, has suffered in turn from the growing spirit of competition which has provided the public with a magnificent station and harbour at Gourock.

Prominent among the old buildings which perished in the widening of East Quay Lane were the old Tontine Stable and a property belonging to Mr. Robert Boag, a gentleman who was a member of the Town Council in the dawning years of the century, and whose name in so honourably associated with the earlier days of Free Education in Greenock. There are incidents associated with the demolition that are now rapidly becoming traditions. There can be but few Greenockians whose recollections extend themselves to the memorable days of Pie Betty, and her once flourishing shop in the now demolished portion of East Quay Lane. Pie Betty, however, lived and thrived half a century ago, and her place of merchandise was much frequented by the Greenock merchants and the gentleman of the time. The attraction seems to have been a double one, the manner and the wares of the fair occupant being alike popular. In short, a fine presence, a superiority of intellect, and a charming geniality of manner, characterised this lady pie-vendor fame, and made her a favourite with the masculine elite among the Greenock folks of fifty years ago. Local tradition relates that a daughter of Pie Betty's became the wife of Captain Jump, a gentleman who was known as a partner of the eminent shipping firm of Duff, MacKinroy & Co. of Liverpool. This Mr MacKinroy at one time occupied Levan House, on the Cloch Road, which became for a time, in recent years, the residence of Mr James Johnston Grieve, ex-Provost of and ex-MP for Greenock, previous to his settling down in Edinburgh.

The East Quay Lane

VII

Glasgow, Paisley, and Greenock Railway Station, 1841

In the removal of this old and much frequented Cathcart Street Station, which took place some three years ago, there has disappeared a conspicuous Greenock landmark. In the accompanying picture we have the front elevation of the building as originally designed and executed in 1841. This picture of the now removed Station Building is more than ordinarily suggestive. It not only sends the mind back half a century in the history of the town, but marks the year 1841 as an epoch making period in the fortunes of the community. The construction of the new line was undertaken by the Glasgow, Paisley and Greenock Railway company, which had been formed for the purpose, and the stock was largely and heartily subscribed for by well-to-do Greenock citizens. The Glasgow and Greenock Railway was opened for traffic on the 31st March 1841. The cost of constructing the new line largely exceeded estimated costs, resulting in great damage to the Greenock company stock and subsequently allowing it to be bought over by Caledonian Railways. The amalgamation of the two companies took place in 1847, just a year previous to the opening of the Caledonian Railway from Carlisle to Edinburgh. The construction of the branch line to Gourock necessitated the demolition of the old landmark at Cathcart street, which has been superseded by a comparatively modern type of building. The new station, if more spacious and magnificent, is not quite so conveniently situated for the public as the old one.

The railway connection, as was to be expected, exercised a favourable influence upon the trade of the town. This is seen in the growth of the population, which in 1841 was under 37,000, or little more than half of what it is today. When the iron horse was introduced the communication between Greenock, Paisley, Glasgow and intervening places was mainly by the river. The old stage coach, which had so long connected the different centres of population throughout the country, and about which so much romance still lingers, was gradually disappearing, and in those districts connected by waterways had all but passed away. When the trains began to run between Greenock and Glasgow there was, on the whole, a not inefficient service of both goods and passenger steamers on the river. Turning to an old directory dated a few years earlier we find a list of the steamers which were plying daily between the lower and upper reaches of the Clyde. These were the Caledonian; Clarence; Greenock; Helensburgh; Sultan; Waverley. There were other small steamers or passage boats sailing regularly from Greenock, which in addition to carrying passengers to Port Glasgow, Dumbarton and Glasgow, called in at Erskine Ferry, Cartmouth and Renfrew. The service of steamers connecting the Clyde with Dublin, Belfast, Liverpool and other parts was considerable, while communication with the coast and places below Greenock was also well maintained.

This picture of the now displaced station, with its vanishing history of half-a-century, vivifies old associations and awakens sleeping memories. There is hardly a limit to the train of thought suggested by the old station, which daily for more than half-a-century received and despatched its living human freight. It was more than a railway terminus; it was also an important rendezvous or public trysting place, the removal of which, while touching most, will hardly affect two individuals alike. To some it will recall joyful, to others sorrowful occasions; not a few will be reminded of kindly genial faces that are seen no more; while to those "afflicted with the malady of thought" it will alter the perspective of life and fill the mind with a series of mellowing reflections.

Glasgow, Greenock and Paisley Railway Station

VIII
The Anchor Inn

The building represented by the accompanying picture, though once instinct with life and passion, is now to the inhabitants of Greenock little more than a name. The Anchor Inn, which has disappeared under the operations of the Improvement Trust, was situated on the south side of Shaw Street, between Highland Close and East Quay Lane; and its origin takes us back to a period of considerable antiquity. It was in existence ere yet the fishing village had developed into modern Greenock; and opening out not on the well-formed harbour of today, but on the beach, was largely frequented by the better class of sea captains and strangers of the time. The building had a fine elevation suggestive of a quiet dignity, and architecturally may be said to have been in advance of its day. On taking down the old building, a west-end gentleman was so impressed with the beauty of some of the architectural ornaments that he requested permission to obtain them. The request being granted, he had them removed to grace the summerhouse in connection with his garden.

The year 1703 is the date at which the Anchor Inn is supposed to have been built, so that it must have long preceded the improved hotel accommodation that was afterwards called into existence by the growth of the community. The Museum Hotel was built about 1750. the White Hart about 1770, and the Tontine in 1801; so that the Anchor Inn is supposed to have been for a long period the leading hotel of the town. The character of the hotel, its general appearance and surroundings were such as to indicate that it had seen better days. It had so deteriorated at the time we speak of that it was utilised for the business of penny reels at the summer fair. The old inn may be said to have witnessed the dawn of the towns development. This is evident when it is recalled that fully half a century after it was built the streets were nameless, with the exception of main thoroughfare, known as the High Street, which extended from the Row or Rue-end to the Kirk Burn, and was the direct route through which passed worshippers from Port-Glasgow and Kilmalcolm to the old West Kirk. The following minute, extracted from the records of the Town Council, dated August 1775, shows the rather embryonic condition of the town at this time;

"...Same day, the meeting considered it necessary that the streets in the town have names to distinguish them from each other - therefore they agreed that the streets after described should be called as follows: The Laigh Street, from Row-end to the Midequay, to be called Shaw Street; from the Midequay to the Bridge, Dalrymple Street; from Row-end to the Square, Cathcart street; the street from the Square westward, Hamilton Street; from the Square to the Midequay, William Street..."

It is thus 116 years since street designation was adopted in Greenock. On the opposite side of the street, and a little to the west of the site of the Anchor Inn, still stands an old property, which forms the corner of Cross-Shore Street. Considerable interest attaches to this old tenement, part of which was at one time occupied as an inn, which is believed to have been the local terminus of the stage coach in the days before the advent of steamers and railways. The date (1716) is still legible on the front of the building, and the Inn in connection therewith must have been of considerable importance when Shaw and Dalrymple Streets formed the main highway of Greenock. The locality here is rather historical. At the junction of Cross-shore and Shaw Streets, there was four stones in the form of a cross, indicating the place were goods and chattels were sold by public roup. Near by, at the foot of Cross-shore Street, on the Breast, were situated the Tar Pots, which were used in old times by carpenters and others while graving vessels on the bank or shallow part of the harbour during low tides. The smell at times was a little disagreeable to the olfactory nerves of passers by. An old bookstall stood not far off, where many of our older readers may have picked up bargains.

The Anchor Inn

IX
Shaw Street, South Side
From Cross-shore Street, looking west.

That portion of Shaw Street, to the immediate west of Cross-shore Street, as it exists to-day, is in striking and pleasing contrast with previous features of the district, as represented by the accompanying view. The south side of Shaw Street, running westwards from Cross-shore Street to William Street, has been entirely re-built. Many of the displaced structures were at one time important both as business premises and as private residences. In the immediate locality represented by the picture were the Old Town House and lock-up. Previous to the recent removal of the prison in Bank Street, the jail, or "Black Hole" as it was called, was situated in front of the Town House; and it may be mentioned, as stated in Weir's "History of Greenock," that "the first 'durance vile' which was used in Greenock was a thatched house at the bottom of Broad Close, where the jugs (or jougs) were hung *in terrorum* of offenders." This was a primitive method for the temporary detention and punishment of sturdy beggars and other offenders, by which they were attached to the outside of the prison walls, and subjected to the ignominy of public exposure.

There was also in the immediate vicinity a much-frequented tavern, in which many of the Council meetings were held, an evidence surely that the dignity surrounding the Town Councillor of to-day was unknown to his predecessor of the olden time. The building in which the business of the tavern was carried on is still extant, and is at present the property of Mr. Edward McCallum, who has a grocery establishment in the low flat.

Shaw Street, South Side From Cross-shore Street, looking west.

X
Broad Close

This view brings before us the Broad Close of a quarter of a century ago. It is, despite its name, a narrow thoroughfare, running parallel with Highland Close, and connecting Cathcart with Shaw Street. Previous to 1858, the ancient structure on both sides of the close had undergone little alteration; but with the erection, at this date, of the City Buildings, which form the south-eastern portion of the lane, a great improvement took place. In 1877, the School Board erected Shaw Street public seminary, which forms the north-eastern portion, with the result that the whole east side of the Broad Close has been entirely modernised. The west side consists of the Tontine buildings, erected at the beginning of the century, and other older structures.

On this side of the Close there still stands an old building, part of which was utilised as the Star Hall. This hall for many years formed the district mission premises of the Free Middle Church; and it is worthy of record that, long before the passing of the compulsory education act, this congregation had in vigourous operation here, not only religious, but educational schemes for the benefit of the district. They instituted a day school in the Star Hall, which was known as the Broad Close School, in which a sound education was provided for the children of the district at nominal fees. The first teacher of the Broad Close School was Mr. W. McCall, of Newton-in-Ayr, who was appointed in 1857. Mr. Gordon Simpson, at present headmaster of Ann Street Public School, taught there from 1866 to 1874, and it is worthy of remark that he was the first teacher in Greenock in possession of a Government certificate, and the first under the Greenock School Board to earn the Government grant.

The Broad Close School disappeared with the erection of Shaw Street Public Seminary, which made provision on an adequate scale for the educational wants of the district. The mission premises of the Free Middle Church are now in the Arcade Hall. Mr. John Malcolm at one time carried on a printing business in the Broad Close. This gentleman, it will be remembered, was subsequently appointed Inspector of Poor for Greenock, an office which he held for many years, when he was succeeded by the present inspector, Mr. John S. Deas.

Broad Close

XI
Longwell Close

The Longwell Close, around which some of the earlier associations of Greenock clustered, is no longer known as such. It was a narrow passage running parallel with William Street, and connecting Cathcart Street with Shaw Street. The Close was one of the condemned areas under the operation of "The Artizans' Dwellings Act," and the dilapidated tenements on both sides have given place to better and more sanitary erections. It has been converted into a modern thoroughfare, which has been designated Duff Street, in complimentary recognition of the services rendered by the late Bailie John Duff to the Improvement Trust, of which he was for many years the convenor. The citizen, whose memory is perpetuated by the new street, was a son of Provost Duff, who presided over the destinies of Greenock some thirty years ago, and a brother of Dr. David Duff, Professor of Church History in the United Presbyterian Church, whose recent death has been so much regretted. The Longwell Close derived its name from a deep well believed to have been built on the property of James Johnstone, situated in the locality, which is supposed to have come into existence two hundred years ago. Referring to this well, Mr. George Williamson, in his second volume of "Old Greenock," remarks, at page 32 :-

"Tradition says the well is 'deep,' like that of Jacob, mentioned by the Evangelist St. John, and so frequently described by travellers in the Holy Land, and whose fame has lasted, and will last, for ages. Some old residenters assert that the Longwell is fifty, others, sixty feet deep. This we can well credit. It is satisfactory to state that in the course of the operations of the Improvement Trust in removing the old houses in the Close for the formation of what is now known as Duff Street a deep well has been discovered which fully answers the description above given. In digging a trench for the common sewer in the middle of the street, a well was discovered about two feet under the causeway. It proved to have been built without lime, and measured exactly four feet six inches in diameter, so that its circumference must have been not less than thirteen feet. The eastern portion had been accidentally removed in the course of excavation, but the western half was intact. It had been filled up and covered with large water-rolled stones. On endeavouring to fathom the depth of the well the workmen put down a boring-rod seventeen feet in length, and found no bottom. When the rod was drawn up, the water 'sprang,' it was said, 'to the surface,' proving that it was supplied by a spring. Can it be doubted that the fine cool spring water was highly-prized as an essential ingredient of the famous punch, consumed by the Bailies, Councillors, and other citizens of the olden time in the adjoining tap-room, or in the taverns of McLeran, McDougall, Mrs. Gordon, Mrs. Reid, Mrs. Alexander, and others frequented by the Magistrates and Council, and the citizens generally."

In forming the new street care has been taken to mark the site of the famous Old Well. In entering Duff Street, there may be observed, midway between Cathcart and Shaw Streets, a large circular stone in the middle of the thoroughfare containing the following inscription: "The Long Well, 1682." The Close was not much of a thoroughfare, except for those living in the locality, which were of the poorer class.

Longwell Close

XII

Dalrymple Street from William Street looking west, showing the James Watt Inn

The adjacent picture represents the place, and also what was popularly believed to be the veritable house in which James Watt was born. The site is now vacant, the tenement having disappeared, along with many others, in the course of the renovation process that has taken place in Greenock. The house, as here represented, was the second tenement from the South West corner of William Street, where it was intersected by Dalrymple Street. It was not, however, the actual house in which the infant Watt first drew the breath of life. The original structure which had been hallowed by the birth of the mighty genius that was to transform the world, was removed towards the end of the last century. At that time Mrs Helen Cameron, or Cambridge, purchased the premises and rebuilt the house where, in 1736, the boy whose early youth and mature manhood were to be engaged in devising cunning appliances for harnessing the steam giant to the service of man, came into existence. In the introduction to "Memorials of James Watt," the writer says;

"A first and essential point was to discover, if possible, the house in which Mr. Watt was born. This was soon satisfactorily done. It was ascertained upon the evidence, both oral and documentary, that James Watt first drew the breath of life in a house which had stood upon the site of the tenement occupied in part, in 1820 as the 'Greenock Tavern'. The old, or original house fronted the sea, from which it was removed only by the breadth of an ordinary road, in process of time called the High Street, and afterwards, as it is at present, Dalrymple Street. The tenement in question is the last but one at the eastern termination of the south side of Dalrymple Street."

The Greenock Tavern, in its later years, was better known as the James Watt Inn; and it is interesting to state that it was, during election times, the headquarters of one or other of the local parties striving for municipal or parliamentary honours; and was frequently, for weeks preceding an election during the days of the restricted franchise, kept as an open house for the voters. James Watt was born in 1736, and died in 1819, at the advanced age of 83. He was buried in Parish Church of Heathfield, at Handsworth, where a Gothic chapel, enshrining a marble statue by Chantrey, was shortly afterwards erected to his memory. His father and immediate "forbears" lie in the Old West Kirk burying-ground. Greenock as yet has but little to boast of as regards the architectural or the monumental, and so far she has no adequate public memorial to perpetuate the fame of her great and distinguished son. People of many lands have offered contributions towards a memorial, and it can only be a question of time when a fitting monument will arise to perpetuate the fame of James Watt. A leading local engineer and shipbuilder has signified his willingness to subscribe the sum of two hundred pounds as the nucleus of a fund towards the erection of a memorial in William Street, provided the town would make a gift of the vacant site. But, so far as can be gathered, the times are not yet ripe for such action on the part of the authorities. In the meantime the Greenock corporation are in the possession of a priceless heritage, from which no sordid considerations should permit their alienation. Whatever may be done in other parts of the town to show honour to the memory of Watt, the site of is birthplace should be guarded with a loving care, and transformed into an artistic and beautiful memorial that would be at once a rallying centre for strangers, and a worthy recognition of the eminent citizen who was cradled in our midst.

Dalrymple Street from William Street

XIII
The Bell Entry

To bye gone generations there was, perhaps, no locality in town better known than that represented by the accompanying picture. The old and historical building known as the Bell Entry has, in common with many others, been sacrificed to the sanitary and architectural requirements of the time. It fronted the West Harbour, near the foot of the Vennel, and in its day was a conspicuous centre of activity and local interest. A part of it still remains, but its value as a venerable landmark has been destroyed. The grand old building has been cut in two, with the result that the western portion has been removed.

The origin of the building, formerly known as the Town Cellars, and afterwards designated The Bell Entry, is exceedingly interesting, as throwing a valuable side-light on the development of the town's trade during the latter part of the eighteenth century. Tobacco and other imports had been increasing, and the Town Council of the time were memorialised by Glasgow and Greenock merchants to provide additional warehouse accommodation. The result was the erection of the Town Cellars, which took place about 1750. The site of the new warehouses was for very many years one of the busiest portions of the town. It is interesting to note how the designation of the Bell Entry was given to the building, and how it gradually superseded that of the Town Cellars. The workmen employed about the West Harbour feeling the want of a clock to indicate the time, and a bell to summon them to and from work, requested the Council of the day to furnish these requirements. The following minute of Council, dated 5th November, 1754, shows that the local rulers of the time were not averse to granting the workmen's request.

"As the triangles whereon the bell is hung in the Royal Closs are so much decayed that it is necessary they be removed, it was proposed that a Bellhouse be erected upon the roof of the New Cellars, to be executed as that a clock may be placed therein, into which Bellhouse the said bell in the Royal Closs may be hung."

The result was the erection of a Bell-Tower above the passage or archway through the building, which was duly furnished with clock and bell. (The bell, however, was a new one, as that taken from the Royal Closs was found to be too small for the new belfry.) Hence arose the name of the Bell Entry, by which the Town Cellars were afterwards known. The steeple of the Mid Parish Church was not erected till 1787, previous to which time that at the Bell Entry was the only spire in town. The bell and clock at the Entry were in use up till 1839, in which year the timber steeple or belfry having become dangerous was taken down. The bell in the Old West Kirk was the first in Greenock; the second was in the Royal Closs; and the third was that hung in the timber steeple at the Bell Entry. It is not known what became of the bell at the Entry; but it will interest not a few to learn that the original bell of the Old West Kirk is still doing duty in Greenock. It is located in the belfry of the West Parish Church, where it is used for striking the quarters of the hour. It is thus an important link between the old kirk and the new, and a relic that can hardly fail to be appreciated in this memorable year of West Parish retrospection.

In the east-end of the Bell Entry building there was a loft, which was converted into a Chapel for the Seamen's Friends' Society. Previous to this, services for seamen were held on board a vessel in the harbour. The Seamen's Friends' Society have now their well-equipped Sailor's Home, with Chapel and Reading-Room, at East India Breast. Immediately adjoining the Bell Entry was a famous tap room or public-house, of which Mr. John Farquhar, and afterwards Mr. Hugh Blair, were for many years the genial landlords. It was a place of much resort, and in the earlier years of the century was largely frequented by West-end youths. There must still, we should suppose, be among us a few survivals of the time when the tavern in connection with the Bell Entry could boast of its being a popular rendezvous or trysting-place, familiarly known as "Philippi." In the first half of the century it was not customary to exact social penalties for frequenting public-houses; and it was not uncommon among Greenock gentlemen, when saying "*Au revoir*" to their friends, to add "I shall see thee again at Philippi." The old Dry Dock, beside the Bell Entry, the first of the kind constructed on Greenock, was built by subscription in 1780.

The Bell Entry

XIV
The House with Five Gables

The house with the five gables, as portrayed in the accompanying picture, was a quaint specimen of architecture that takes us back to the seventeenth century. It was a common architectural feature of the earlier part of that period; and buildings of corresponding design are still to be met with in Cartsdyke, and in the older parts of the City of Edinburgh.

The house of which we herewith give a representation was situated in Dalrymple Street, at the east corner of Taylor's Close, and, in common with many others, has perished with the progress of the Improvement Trust. Behind the five gabled land shown in the illustration was a court called Jibboom Square. It was irregularly formed, and was surrounded by two-storied houses. In connection with these tenements, there were four distinct outside stairs, each of which consisted of from 12 to 14 steps, with wooden hand rails or ravels leading to the respective houses. The locality was so disreputable that respectable citizens would hardly dream of entering it after sundown.

In certain old houses in Dalrymple Street and in Cartsdyke there has been observed a rather singular feature. This was a small square of glass or solitary window-pane inserted in some of the old-fashioned gables, in direct communication with the chimney. It has been supposed that this peculiar arrangement was designed to reflect the light of the fire for the benefit of fishing-boats coming in from the sea. The contrivance, however, is believed to have served a double purpose. In many of the old houses referred to, the windows were so placed that no light from them could reach the fireplace; and it is thought that the streak of daylight coming through the square of glass at the back of the chimney was intended to facilitate the cooking operations of the housewife by day, as well as to guide the movements of the fishermen by means of a lamp at night. The house with the five gables must at one time have faced the beach, and had this singular feature of chimney or gable light to which we have referred.

The House with Five Gables

XV
Lindsay's Lane

This picture gives us an interesting view of Lindsay's Lane, which in the earlier days of Greenock was rather an important business quarter of the town. Opening from West Quay Lane, and running eastwards in parallel line with the harbour, it terminates with the Vennel, into which it forms an outlet. In Lindsay's Lane and West Breast there are still extant some old properties with important historical associations. The offices of the Greenock Custom House were located there, and immediately adjoining was the Greenock Bank.

It was not till 1714 that Greenock was declared a public port; and in that year officers of Her Majesty's Customs from Port Glasgow were stationed here for the collection of revenue. There is no distinct evidence to fix the exact situation of the first Custom House opened in Greenock, but it is generally supposed to have been in Cathcart street. It is known, however, that the business of Her Majesty's Customs in Greenock was for many years transacted on the first floor of a tenement at the east corner of William Street and Mid Quay. These offices were leased by the Commissioners of Customs in 1759; and there the business of this public department continued to be carried on till the closing years of the century, when it was transferred to Bailie Gammell's property in Lindsay's Lane. Here the offices continued until the erection of the handsome Greenock Custom House fronting the Old Steamboat Quay, the foundation stone of which was laid on the 2nd of May, 1817.

The old Greenock Bank, the history of which is so closely associated with Lindsay's Lane and West Breast, was established one hundred and six years ago and had a career of fifty eight years, after which it became absorbed in the Western Bank. At the centenary celebration of the Watt Library, held 5th January, 1883, Mr John Scot, C.B., in an address reviewing the growth of Greenock during the hundred years that had elapsed since the opening of the library, stated, that some spirited individuals in our neighbourhood had established Greenock's first bank in 1785, under the name of Dunlop, Houstoun, Gammell & Co., which was afterwards better known as the Greenock Bank, several guinea notes of which were to be seen in the Museum. The Mr. Gammell who figured in the co-partnery of the Greenock Bank was Bailie James Gammell, of Garvel Park, who built and owned the property in Lindsay's Lane in which the Custom House and the Bank were located. He died in 1825. The late Mr Alexander Thomson, so well and so favourably known as a citizen and a banker, entered the service of the Greenock Bank in 1800. Mr Thomson had been only eighteen months in the Greenock office when he was promoted to the management of the Bank.

The Greenock Bank continued to exist till 1843, when its business was purchased by the Western Bank, and absorbed in the larger concern. It was the last private Bank of issue in Scotland. At this time the manager, Mr Alexander Thomson, was one of the principal shareholders. He was a native of the parish of Killin, and died in 1867, at the advanced age of ninety. In the early years of the century, he had built the stately mansion of Caddlehill. We have still happily with us a representative of the Thomson family in the person of Mr James Thomson, who occupies the family residence at Caddlehill, and who in going out and in among us brightens our daily life with his genial manner and his interesting reminiscences of our earlier Greenock times. The one guinea notes of the Greenock Bank may still be seen in the Watt Museum. To these a rather tragic interest attaches, as they were found with other valuables on the body of a passenger who had met his doom through the disaster to the "Comet," which was run down off Gourock by the steamer "Ayr" in 1825. The well known robbery of the Greenock Bank, which was effected by London thieves took place from the Assembly Room Buildings on the 9th March, 1828.

Lindsay's Lane

XVI
Cathcart Square and "Cowan's Corner"

Cathcart Square, so familiar to present-day Greenockians, has been from time immemorial the historical centre of the town. The active and busy generations now no more have often demonstrated within its precincts giving expression of their approval or disapproval of the men and measures of the time. The Fairs of the olden time were exclusively held within its area, and here the showmen of the past harangued the crowd on the cheapness and the excellence of their tinsel wares. Here, twice a year, assembled from the surrounding districts, farmers and their wives, and agricultural servants, male and female, the former in quest of men and maids, and the latter on the lookout for masters and mistresses, the result being a motly crowd and a curious huckstering as to fees, accompanied by extraordinary scenes of jollity and mirth.

It is worthy of note that Greenock, which had taken a prominent part in the agitation leading up to the Reform Act of 1832, held an imposing demonstration on the passing of the Bill, one incident of which was the burning of a ship's boat in Cathcart Square. The Mid Parish Church has looked down upon the square for 129 years, it having been first opened for public worship in 1761, the congregation of the Mid Parish previously meeting in the Royal Closs Loft. The buildings forming the immediate environment of the Square have been within comparatively recent years the subject of considerable change. What is now known as Forrest's Land still remains intact and rises majestically on the north side, it being now occupied as the emporium of the enterprising Messrs. Rowan. But we miss the Temperance Hotel, once known as Mann's, and subsequently as Buchanan's, immediately adjoining Cowan's Corner. On ceasing to be occupied as a hotel, it was for some time utilised as the offices of the Water Trust and the Sanitary Department. The building forming the north-west corner of Hamilton Street and Cathcart Square, occupied by Messrs. Robert Cowan & Co., is now also looked for in vain. The removed structures have all perished under the operations of the Improvement Trust. In the premises which have now acquired the historical designation of "Cowan's Corner," Messrs. Robert Cowan & Co. carried on an extensive drapery business; and the popularity of the firm is worth recording. Its reputation for substantial goods, integrity of business dealing, and courtesy in customers, rich and poor alike, was such that it attracted not only the town's people, but country folks from far and near.

The original plans of the Municipal Buildings covered the site of the Messrs. Cowan's premises, and, on the understanding that it was to be also utilised, the firm had to remove; and now carry on their business at the north corner of West Blackhall and West Burn Streets. The historical Coffee Room, one of the most interesting features of Cathcart Square, is still with us, but it is not likely to have a much longer lease, as it is marked out for absorption in the contemplated extension of the premises of the British Linen Banking Company.

Cathcart Square and "Cowan's Corner"

XVII
The Old Town Offices

This picture represents the modest suite of offices for transacting the towns business as existing up til 1880. Entering from the north side of Hamilton Street, a few yards west from Cathcart Square, through a wide passage, found himself in close proximity to the Chamberlains office and that of the collector of assessments; while above, in a portion of the Old Town Hall were located the Town Clerk and his subordinates, with the office of the Harbour Trust in the immediate vicinity. Access was also obtained to the old Police Court from this passage, which led in to the new and present Town Hall. The fate of these familiar and time honoured places was sealed by a resolution of the Corporation in 1878 to provide office accomodation that would better serve the convenience of the public and be more in keeping with the dignity of the town. To Provost Lyle and his colleagues of 1878 belong the honour of initiating the erection of the splendid pile of Municipal Buildings, which has done so much to redeem the architectural reputation of Greenock. The unfortunate failure of the authorities to acquire "Cowan's Corner" has made it impossible to complete the original, an accident which - if ever repaired - is more likely to be accomplished in the remote rather than the near future. The Victoria Tower, which rises to a height of 230 feet commands from its summit an extensive and magnificent view, and renders the building conspicuous to those passing up and down the river. The entire cost of the municipal buildings is £200,000, a sum very considerably in excess of the original estimates.

With the erection of the new buildings there have disappeared the old Town Offices and numerous eyesores in that quarter of the town. The result is that we not only have a magnificent block of Corporation Buildings, but a large and central district of the town converted from an insanitary into a sanitary area, an advantage so great that it cannot be measured by a money value.

It will easily be remembered that the 6th August 1881 was a memorable day in the annals of Greenock. On that date the town was the scene of an imposing demonstration taking the form of a trades procession during the day and a banquet in the Town Hall in the evening. The occasion served a double purpose, at once celebrating the laying the foundation stone of the Municipal Building and that of the James Watt Dock. The important local event attracted eminent persons from a distance to grace the ceremonial occasion of which Provost Cambell was the central and commanding figure.

The removal of the Old Town offices was effected in 1880; and with them there disappeared another landmark in the history of the community. There are those who see in the removal of old fabrics nothing but the displacement of so much material, but there are others, more highly organised, whose quick sympathies and poetic imaginations enable them to re-people the vacant places with the human forms that dwelt therein. Such sensitively alive to the lessons of the historical, surround themselves with the associations of long ago, which emphasise the transitoriness of affairs and engender feelings of considerateness towards those still engaged in the "conflict and the strife".

We are not old enough to remember many of the officials who were accustomed to work and flit about the offices at Hamilton Street, and The Old Town Offices are now a thing of the past, but there are memories connected with them which will lovingly linger in the minds of not a few surviving citizens.

The Old Town Offices

XVIII
Taylor's Close
West Side, From Hamilton Street

The view herewith recalls scenes and sights that were familiar previous to the construction of the magnificent pile known as the Municipal Buildings, and the formation of Wallace Square.

Whatever worthy memories have clustered round the original history of Taylor's Close, there is no doubt that in its later stages its features and associations were not of the loveliest. There is, in connection with the earlier history of the Close, a rather notable incident, and from the names of persons that figure in the story it will be seen that the time of its occurence is still a long way on this side of antiquity.

A workman named Scott, who lived in Taylors Close, was suspected to have broken the law, and a sergeant of police, with the view of arresting him, forced his dwelling without a warrant. Scott, whatever he may have been in other respects was not without intelligence, and he therupon requested the officer to produce his warrant of arrest. The only response vouchsafed to Scott by the sergeant was that "his warrant was the *buckle of his hat*". This was too much for the intended police victim, who, rushing upon his would-be apprehender with a poker, committed a serious asault. For this Scott was brought to trial in Greenock before Sheriff Hercules Robertson, the case, from its nature, attracting a vast amount of interest. The public sympathy was with Scott, who was acquitted ; and the case was rendered memorable by the famous deliverance of the Sheriff, the keynote of which was, from first to last, that a citizens home was an absolute asylum; and that, unless when constitutionally entered, a Briton's house must be regarded as his castle. Scott, it may be remarked, was throughout this remarkable local trial eloquently defended by the late well-known and able Greenock lawyer, Mr James Dunlop.

Taylor's Close

XIX
Old Police Buildings
Taylor's Close

This view gives, among other things, a glimpse of the Old Police Buildings, which were in use from the middle of the century til within the last few years. They formed a plain and unpretentious looking structure fronting Taylor's Close with an entrance from Hamilton Street. The buildings were erected about 1850 to meet the growing requirements of the period; but latterly the cell accomodation provided was declared by Government authority to be unsatisfactory.

The old buildings have been removed and there is now ample and superior police accomodation in that portion of the new Municipal Buildings entering from Dalrymple Street. The old Police Buildings were designed by the Master of Works of the time, The late Mr. William Allison, who was also the architect of the present Town Hall.

Old Police Buildings

XX
The Low Vennel

The accompanying sketch furnishes a view of what once constituted the Low Vennel, with a prospect opening on the harbour. This district of the town - at one time a centre of dilapidated tenements and old rookeries - has in recent years undergone quite a transformation. The space is now occupied, from Hamilton Street to what is now Wallace Square, with buildings erected by the Improvement Trust and the New Post Office.

The formation of Wallace Square may be said to have given a new lung to this part of the town; and it is to be hoped that in an early future, when more prosperous times shall have replenished the Corporation Exchequer, it may be rendered more beautiful and artistic than at present.

The Low Vennel

XXI
The Old Greenock Prison

The old Prison, one of Greenock's ancient landmarks, situated in lower Bank Street, and immediately adjoining the Mid Parish Church was demolished in 1886 to make room for the Caledonian line to Gourock. It was a strongly built house, and many of the stones were in such an excellent state of preservation that they were used by the Railway Company in the construction of walls and bridges.

The old Jail conatined two iron cells for the incarceration and refractory of troublesome prisoners, and it is significant to note, as shewing the harsher methods of former times, that in one of these cells there were ring bolts in the floor with a chain in the wall. Spinning had at one time been the prescribed work of the prisoners, and in removing the old structure, the machinery used for this purpose was discovered. There was further disclosed the remains of an ingenious automatical contrivance by means of which the Governor of the Prison could ascertain the amount of work done by the inmates, and also the precise hour at which they ceased operations.

The associations of the Old Greenock Prison are anything but inspiring, but it may be mentioned that in one of the two iron cells referred to there was confined a man named John Kerr, the first criminal ever executed in Greenock for murder. During the progress of removing the old building workmen came upon the remains of John Boyd, a Greenock man, who had been executed for the murder of his wife in 1835. His body had been interred within the prison, in terms of the death sentence.

As compensation for the old building the Town received from the Caledonian Railway Company the sum of £9000. The Old Prison had been superseded for many years by the superior cell accomodation attatched to the new Court-House in Nelson Street. The old jail or Bridewell as it used to be called, was built in 1810, and in form its appearance resembled an old castle, having two towers in front with battlements at the top.

The Old Greenock Prison

XXII
Old Slaughter House Lane

This view of the Slaughter House Lane reminds us of an incident that is not without historical significance. In its immediate vicinity there was situated the original Ragged School of Greenock, taught by Mr McKellar. The institution was afterwards removed to premises almost immediately behind the Tontine; and it may interest some to know that here that well known Greenock character who went by the name of "Tag-Tag" received his education.

In front of the Slaughter House Lane there was a soap and candle works, carried on by Mr John Ferguson, a well known Town Councillor and keen local politician. This gentleman was a brother of the Messrs. Ferguson, who, some thirty years ago, were known as sugar refiners in Greenock.

Old Slaughter House Lane

XXIII
The Old West Brig

The subject of this picture, though removed many years ago in the interests of town improvement will be easily recognised. The bridge was a veritable landmark situated in a central and busy thoroughfare. At this part of the town there is quite a junction of streets, no fewer than four converging upon one another. These are; West Burn Street - from which the old bridge derived its name - along with Kilblain and Inverkip streets, the west end of the High Vennel, and a lane connecting the locality of Princes Street. Elder Greenockians will recognise in the site of the Auld Brig, as it appears today, a striking contrast to its features of many years ago, as reproduced in the accompanying illustration. One does not require to be very old to remember the mill dam on the upper side of the bridge, the sluices and troughs connected with the wheel of an adjoining industry and the frequent spectacle of children, in summer weather, wading and gambolling in the water. The open nature of the burn at this busy and populous centre having become dangerous and insanitary, it was covered up.

The works that had sprung up on both sides of the burn in the olden time have disappeared; but a few of such are still within the recollection of the older inhabitants. The old mill was taken down in 1860 and on its site there now stands a modern store or warehouse, presently occupied by Mr John Chalmers, grain and potato merchant. The business of the old meal mill was transferred to Bogle Street. To the south east of the bridge was the old logwood or chipping mill which has been removed.

The impounding of the burn at its source by the Shaws Water Company reduced the quantity of water available for manufacturing purposes; and this, along with the impurities generated by sugar refining processes, necessitated the removal of certain industries such as dye works to ther neighbourhoods. In the immediate vicinity, at the extreme west-end of the High Vennel, was a hat manufactory. It is evident that the banks of the West Burn must at the one time have been a veritable hive of industry. It is worthy of note that whereas in 1855 there were six milling establishments in Greenock, that important local industry has considerably dwindled.

The Old West Brig

XXIV
The Old West Kirk
Previous to Restoration

This picture impels our thoughts in the direction of very long ago. The venerable structure which it represents came into existence so far back as three centuries; and around it there gathers the earlier ecclesiastical history of Greenock. This is the more easily understood when it is remembered that up til 1741, the year in which the Mid Parish Church was built, The Old West Kirk was the one and only place of worship in Greenock and its immediate neighbourhood. In the course of excavations in different parts of the town there have been evidences of previous chapels that have perished, and of adjoining graveyards that had fallen into disuse. These chapels or churches however, are supposed to have been swept away amidst the general wreck of religious houses at the time of the Reformation.

The Old West Kirk was opened in 1591 and previous to that time Greenockians who attended divine ordnances had to travel every Sabbath six weary miles over bad roads and dangerous rivulets, to the Church of Innerkip, or, as it was anciently known, The Parish of Daff. The erection of The West Kirk here pictured, obviated this great inconvenience, enabling the people of the time to worship within their own borders. It was situated on the east end of The Glebe and stood in the midst of an extensive burial ground. It was built nearly in the form of a cross, and had a small belfry on the West Side. It is supposed that from The Old West Kirk belfry the sound of a bell first reached the ear of the Greenock people and up till 1789 it was made to ring out its sweetest chimes on joyous occasions, and its mournful peals when a distinguished Greenock citizen was being carried to his long home. In 1829, Weir, the first historian of Greenock, thus comments upon the Kirks adjoining burial ground. "In wandering through the churchyard, there is but little to attract the eye which is not common to every burial ground; and Greenock possesses but few illustrious dead over whose graves we would be apt to linger with emotions of regret. Yet here, unnoticed and scarcely known, is now mouldering in silent dust, Highland Mary, the object of Burn's purest and most exalted attachment, and the theme of his finest effusions. Here also the father of the illustrious James Watt reposes in peace. And here you are reminded of that awful calamity, the sinking of The Comet on the 21st October 1825, by observing the grave which contains Sir Joseph Radcliffe's servants who perished on that awful occasion."

In 1838, The West Kirk was condemned as unfit for occupancy, and, consequent on its abandonment, a new church was declared necessary. The result was the erection of the handsome new structure in Nelson Street, a consumation which was largely brought about through the influence and instrumentality of Dr McFarlan. To the West Parish congregation Dr McFarlan ministered with great acceptance until 1843, the date of the memorable Disruption, when he cast his lot in with the Free Church. The result was the erection of the new Free West Church on the isle of the present Wesleyan Chapel in Ardgowan Street, of which Dr McFarlan became pastor.

In 1846 a movement was set on foot which resulted in the entire renovation of The Old West Kirk. Quite a succession of generations have come and gone, with their chequered lives of joy and sorrow during the three centuries that have elapsed since the erection of The Old West Kirk and while in its happy restoration we recognise the blending of the new and the beautiful with a fitting and becoming reverence for the old, we are alive to the eloquent lesson of its founders, that the consolations of religion which were necessary for them, are equally so for their descendants.

The Old West Kirk

XXV
Highland Mary's Grave

"Oh, Mary! dear departed shade!
Where is thy place of blissful rest?"

There is but little in Greenock to attract the worshippers of the antique, but there is happily one sacred spot, consecrated to love and genius, that constitutes a shrine. Beneath the place marked by the monument repose the ashes of the Highland girl whose memory evoked the sweetest music from the poetic genius of Burns, and whose tender associations are now imperishably blended with the ever widening fame of Scotland's Bard. The stone that marks the resting place of Highland Mary stands at the extreme west portion of the old West Kirk Burying Ground. It is now a veritable shrine towards which strangers from all parts of the world wend their way in ever increasing numbers to pay their devotions. The monument, which owes its existence to public subscription, was erected in 1842. It had been somewhat neglected for years, but it is now under the loving care of the Greenock Burns Club. Her family originally belonged to Dunoon, but subsequently went to Campbeltown, where her father, who had been the master of a sloop, or trading vessel, died and was buried. The family afterwards migrated to Greenock, taking up their residence in the top flat of that house still forming the north-east corner of High Vennel and Sir Michael Street. Mr. Archibald Campbell, of 29 Bank street, Greenock, a nephew of Highland Mary, is still happily to the fore, and has laid us under obligation by supplying us with valuable and definite information gleaned within the range of his own personal experience. Our courteous and kindly informant, though in his 78th year, is still blessed with a clear and retentive memory, and he can easily recall the early years of his boyhood, some of which were spent with his grandmother (Highland Mary's mother) in Sir Michael Street. He has often heard the story of Highland Mary's death referred to, and his statement thereanent is quite in consonance with what is already well known. The wife of Peter Macpherson, a carpenter residing at 31 Upper Charles Street, was a relative of the Campbells, and Mary's brother coming to Greenock as an apprentice carpenter to Messrs. Scott, shipbuilders, took lodgings at her house. He was seized with fever, which was then rife in the district, and his sister, now known as Highland Mary, came to Greenock in order to nurse him; and in turn was laid down with the disease, which issued in a fatal illness. As to the identification of the precise locality in which the Macphersons lived, there can hardly be any mistake, as the testimony of Highland Mary's surviving nephew, based in personal recollection, is clear and strong. As a boy he was frequently sent by his grandmother in Sir Michael street to point out to strangers the house of the Macphersons in Charles Street where her celebrated daughter died. Highland Mary's mother and her two brothers were buried in Duncan Street burying ground. The titles to the lairs in which they are interred are in the possession of Mr. Archibald Campbell, Bank Street, Greenock. As to the woeful blank in the literary heritage we have received from Burns, caused by the absence of the poet's letters and verses to Highland Mary, it is a melancholy satisfaction to know that they were destroyed by a member of the Campbell family doubtless under the honest but erroneous impression that disgrace rather than credit was to be gained by connection with the poet. The loss of the correspondence is much to be lamented, but it is well to remember that in our day we are surrounded by a more liberal mental atmosphere, which enables us to realise the greatness of Burns, and our indebtedness to him in a manner impossible to those who lived in the first half of the century. We are now within five years of the centenary of Burns' death, and still his fame rolls on with an ever-increasing momentum. It is safe to say that as his teaching becomes better understood and more assimilated, the cause of human brotherhood will progress and prosper. Let us rejoice as citizens of Greenock that we are closely associated with persons and places that relate us to the gifted singer that gave a new voice to the better impulses of his Scottish countrymen, and an all-time utterance to the higher aspirations of the race. It may be mentioned that the monument in the Old West Kirk burying-ground, which graces and guards the resting-place of Highland Mary, was the successful outcome of a movement initiated by the Greenock Foresters' Society. The monument was unveiled in 1842, and on that occasion there was a Burns demonstration which took the form of a trades procession.

Highland Mary's Grave

XXVI
The House where Highland Mary Died

"Still o'er these scenes my memory wakes,
And fondly broods with miser care!
Time but the impression stronger makes,
As streams their channels deeper wear.
My Mary! dear departed shade!
Where is thy place of blissful rest?
See'st thou thy lowly lover laid?
Hear'st thou the groans that rend his breast?"

The name and memory of Mary Campbell are now indelibly interwoven with the ever-widening fame of Burns; and Greenock is fortunate enough to possess some consecrated spots invested with all the necessary attractions that constitute a shrine for the admirers of the poet. It was in Greenock that Highland Mary died, and her ashes repose in the Old West Kirk burying-ground. It is touching to observe how jealously public as well as private affections guard the fame, and treasures the associations of the dead that are dear to it. The house in which the loved one dwelt; the familiar places consecrated by his presence; and everything known to have passed through his hands, are regarded with awe and reverence. The slightest thing becomes a cherished relic and an abiding charm. Such an attitude bespeaks the existence of a beautiful trait in human-kind; and when adopted by the public towards their greatest and best shows an appreciation of intellect and heart which exalts our human nature. The house where Highland Mary breathed her last, a victim to a malignant fever, while yet in the bloom of maidenhood, became, as the poet's fame extended, an object of reverence. No definite steps, however, had been taken to identify the spot; and tradition, which is not always reliable or one-voiced, associated it with various localities. It was here, it was there, and it was yonder; but absolute certainty, the one thing needful to satisfy the worshipper of Burns, was still lacking. We are now, however, in a position to state that in associating this house and site with the fatal illness of Mary Campbell, tradition has been astray. The house in which Highland Mary passed away is now no longer in existence. It was situated at 31 Upper Charles Street, on the lefthand side going southwards, and the site is now rebuilt upon. The above picture represents the actual house so closely and so fatally associated with the history of Mary Campbell, and it is hardly necessary to state that the spot on which it stood, along with its surroundings, must ever be dear to all lovers of the poet.

The romantic story of Burns and Highland Mary is well known, but a brief reference to this most interesting passage in the poet's history, along with a statement of the evidence that has enabled us to finally determine the site of the house where Mary Campbell died will, we believe, here find a not inappropriate place. During a time of great despondency, when poverty, in combination with his moral lapses, was supposed to have raised an impenetrable wall between the poet and the Armours, Burns found himself in the society of Mary Campbell, a native of Dunoon, and at the time in domestic service. A sudden but genuine passion sprang up between them; and no one can read the story of their vows and their final parting on the banks of the Ayr, as related in the bard's immortal poem addressed "To Mary in Heaven," without feeling at once the poignant grief that animated the poet's breast, and the empyrean sweep of his lyric genius. The ever-memorable meeting took place on the 14th August, 1786, and the death of Highland Mary took place on the 20th or 21st of the following October. She was born in 1768, so that at the time of her death she was but eighteen years of age.

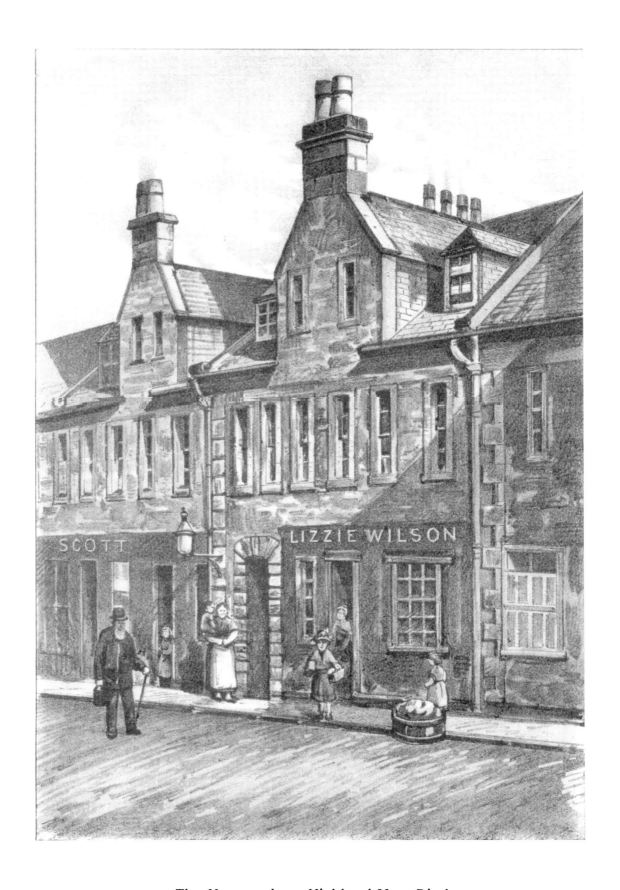

The House where Highland Mary Died

XXVII
Mince Collop Close
Showing House supposed to have been that in which Highland Mary died.

The accompanying picture gives a view of Mince Collop Close, a lane or cul-de-sac now removed. It was situated immediately to the east of William Street, and ran southwards from Shaw Street. It was a disreputable locality, but was rendered not altogether uninteresting on account of the belief that obtained for many years to the fact that it contained the house in which Highland Mary died. The belief, however, was founded on a tradition which later investigation has dispelled. A picture of the actual house where Mary Campbell breathed her last is to be found elsewhere within this volume.

Mince Collop Close

XXVIII
A Bit of West Blackhall Street in 1845

Half a century divides us from the West Blackhall Street of today and that represented by the accompanying illustration. The vista backwards is not too long for some of us to traverse, yet it is more than sufficient to accentuate the transitoriness of life, and the incessant change inseperable from mundane affairs. Elder Greenockians will recollect the house and joiners shop of James Weir, as given in the picture. The premises have been transformed and are now occupied by Mr Ivie Scott and others.

It is only a few years since Mr Weir, a native of Greenock, passed away, and he is still well and kindly remembered in town. Throughout his long life of fourscore years he exhibited a character whose outstanding features were those of kindliness, industry and individuality. We can see him yet, on business bent, as with elastic step he made his way by lane and street, with purpose looking gait, his joiners apron tucked to his side, a hammer suspended therefrom, and glass and putty in hand. Mr James Weir was an enthusiastic collector of old coins and other antiquities.

Opposite Mr Weir's workshop were the extensive sugar stores of Messrs Gray and Buchanan, forming the northwest corner of Argyll Street and West Blackhall Street. It may be remembered that the hogsheads and other sugar packages were hoisted into the lofts by means of horse haulage, and, in order to reach the higher portions of the warehouse, it was necessary for the horses to entirely cross the street. This system of hoistage was common in other parts of the town, but latterly became intolerable in busy thoroughfares such as West Blackhall Street. The obnoxious practice has been superseded by the adoption of excellent hydraulic hoists, now in almost universal use.

Some twenty years ago Messrs Gray and Buchanan disposed of their West Blackhall Street warehouse to Mr Thomas Suttie, then of Greenock, but, now of Aukland, who had it converted into a fine block of shops and offices. It is worthy of note that Mr John Gray, the senior partner of the firm of Gray and Roxburgh, was a gentleman of exquisite taste, and that, as a member of the Council, to him belongs the honour of having designed the walks in our beautiful Greenock Cemetery, the acquisition of which was mainly due to his far-seeing initiative. His son, Mr Hugh Gray, is now living at Helensburgh.

A Bit of West Blackhall Street in 1845

XXIX
The Old Ferry House and the Bay of Quick

There is perhaps none of the sketches of Old Greenock embodied in this memorial volume so thoroughly suggestive of change than that before us. Every Greenockian of the present generation is familiar with the terminus of the Glasgow and South Western Railway and the fine outlet to the river known as Princes Pier; but the citizen who would today revisit his native town after an absence of a quarter century might experience a chilling sensation through failing to recognise his once well known and much frequented Bay of Quick. The form and spirit of the place are new, nought remaining save the natural contour of the river and the beautiful prospect opening out therefrom.

In the pre-steamboat days the ferry was the mode of fording loch and river. That stationed in the Bay of Quick was used to convey people to and from Rosneath and other parts of the Clyde. Previous to the acquisition of the Bay of Quick site for railway purposes, it was mainly occupied as a sawmill and a shipbuilding yard. The mill was owned by Mr John Brown, a gentleman who subsequently acted as editor of the Greenock Herald; while the shipbuilding yard was the property of the late, well known and esteemed local shipbuilder Mr James McMillan. When Mr McMillan had been about eleven years at the Bay of Quick his whole ground and building were scheduled under an act of Parliament, obtained by the Greenock and Ayrshire Railway company, for railway necessities. Mr James McMillan was awarded £2,700 with interest thereon as compensation for his shipbuilding yard.

Any notice of the Bay of Quick which failed to recognise the services of Mr James Johnston Grieve, ex-provost of, and ex-M.P. for Greenock would be to the last degree, defective. Mr Grieve's name is not only indissolubly associated with this quarter of the town, but with the port as a whole. He was one of the leading promoters of the Greenock and Ayrshire Railway; and worthy monuments to his insight, his patriotism and his enterprise are to be found in the Esplanade, the Albert and Victoria harbours, our Gryfe water supplies, and in other schemes for developing the resources of the town. Mr Grieve could see down the avenue of the future, and has virtually ploughed himself into the history of Greenock.

The Old Ferry House and the Bay of Quick

XXX
The Old Highlanders Academy

This popular educational institution, situated in the west-end of Roxburgh Street, was compelled by the exigencies of the Gourock Railway to change its quarters; and the old buildings, which had been in existence for fifty years were taken down in 1887. The Highlander's Academy, originally intended for the education of the children of the poorer Highlanders in the community, was built by voluntary effort, and was the result of a movement that took place in 1834. In that year it was suggested by some members of the Gaelic Chapel that the use of the Gaelic language in the forenoon service should be dispensed with; and the Greenock Highlanders, naturally resenting the innovation, took steps for the better securing alike of the church and school accommodation in accordance with their own traditions and desires. In order to effect this purpose, a society formed; and ultimately - the idea of providing church accommodation being discarded - the attention of the society was concentrated on the erection and endowment of a school for the children of Highlanders in Greenock and vicinity. It was ascertained at that time that there were 2000 adult Highlanders in Greenock, and that 300 of their children required to be sent to school. It was subsequently resolved that a day school should be built, providing accommodation for 400 infants and juveniles.

The foundation stone was laid of the 31st August, 1835, and the Highlanders' Academy was opened in the following year. In 1842, an additional storey was added to a part of the original structure, in order to provide a commercial department. The Academy, though originally denominational in character and constitution, became, after a few years, thoroughly liberalised, and though the original name was retained, it was open to children of all classes of parents, who largely availed themselves of its excellent educational advantages. The moving spirit of erection of the Highlanders' Academy was Mr. Daniel McArthur, who died in 1850. A second additional enlargement was made on the Academy buildings in 1875, which greatly improved the appearance, and provided greater comfort alike for teachers and pupils. In 1881 the school was taken over by the Greenock School Board, and the old associations that clustered round it have been transferred to the handsome new structure in Mount Pleasant Street, which perpetuates the name and associations of the old Highlanders' Academy.

There are numerous persons in and beyond the town whose memories lovingly linger round the old building, whose boyish and girlish days were spent in its well-remembered class rooms and its familiar playground; and by many of these an affectionate regret was expressed at its demolition. It has now, however, to be classed with old Greenock, as of its material part nought remains but the faithful picture now before us.

The Old Highlanders Academy

XXXI
Crow Mount

This picture is interesting as taking us back some fifty years in the history of Greenock. Crow Mount, or, as it was commonly called, the Mount, formed that portion of the town stretching westwards from Bank Street to Ann Street, and running northwards from Dempster Street to Roxburgh Street. At the time referred to it was largely a plantation with a few gardens, and here and there a cottage or residence of some well known citizen. The district represented by the Mount is now covered with dwellings, but fifty years ago it was for the most part unfeued.

Crow Mount was in its way, a miniature forest, with trees of luxuriant growth, which attracted crows, and made it a breeding place and a centre for this well known species of bird, the chorus of whose peculiar cawing became a familiar feature of the neighbourhood and doubtless gave the Mount its name. The pictorial sketch herewith is in striking contrast to the transformation which exists today and is significantly suggestive as to how Greenock in her later years, has outgrown her original boundaries and extended herself into the country.

Among a few well known citizens who had their homes on or about the Mount may be mentioned; the late William Gaff, joiner; Mr Hugh Dempster, writer; Mr Robert Buchanan, cooper ; Captain Robert Cuthbert; and the present Mr Alexander Ranken Johnston. At the junction of Holmscroft and Trafalgar Streets, on what was the central portion of Crow Mount, now stands Mount Park Free Church, which owes its name to the locality. The church, of which the Rev. A.D. Grant is pastor, was opened in 1874.

Crow Mount

XXXII
Castle of Easter Greenock

This view gives a representation of Easter Castle as it lay in ruins at the end of the last century. It was situated about half-a-mile to the south of Cartsdyke, and was for centuries the Mansion-House of Easter Greenock. The old castle, with estates of Eastern Greenock were reunited with the ancient Barony of Greenock in 1669, after a prolonged separation, during which they were in possession of the Crawfurds, of Kilbirny.

The Castle of Easter Greenock

Historical Memoranda

The Following is a Chronicle of Notable Local Events

Greenock Constituted a Burgh of Barony	1635
James Watt Born	1736
Election of First Magistrates and Council	1751
Greenock Library Instituted	1783
First issue of "Greenock Advertiser"	1802
East India Harbour - Foundation Stone Laid	1805
Greenock Infirmary Opened	1809
Greenock Chamber of Commerce Incorporated	1813
Sheriff Court Opened	1815
Flood at Cartsdyke	1815
Greenock Provident Bank Opened	1815
James Watt Died	1819
Greenock Coffee Room Opened	1815
Shaws Water Introduced	1827
First Gaswork Erected	1829
Flood at Cartsdyke	1835
Mechanics Institute - Foundation Stone Laid	1839
Glasgow, Greenock and Paisley Railway Opened	1841
Greenock Cemetery Opened	1846
Victoria Harbour Opened	1850
Sir Gabriel Woods Mariners Home - Foundation Stone Laid	1850
First Issue of "Greenock Herald"	1852
House of refuge Opened	1853
The Wood Asylum Opened	1854
Greenock Academy Opened	1855
Greenock Telegraph newspaper Established	1857
Greenock Ragged School Opened - Captain Street	1858
Greenock Philosophical Society Instituted	1861
Albert Harbour Foundation Stone Laid	1862
First Daily Issue of "Greenock Telegraph"	1863
Wemyss Bay Railway Opened	1865
Albert Harbour Opened	1867
New Court House Opened	1869
Greenock and Ayrshire Railway Opened	1869
Buchanan Night Asylum Opened	1870
Garvel Dock Foundation Stone Laid	1871
Gryffe Water Introduced	1872
Inchgreen Gas Works Opened	1873
Tramway to Gourock Opened	1873
First School Board Elected	1873
Watt Museum Foundation Stone Laid	1875
Watt Museum Opened	1876
Smithson Poorhouse and Asylum Opened	1879
Lyle Road Opened	1880
Ferguson Eye Infirmary Opened	1880
Lyle Road Opened	1880
Ferguson Eye Infirmary Opened	1880
James Watt Dock Opened	1886
Railway to Gourock Opened	1889

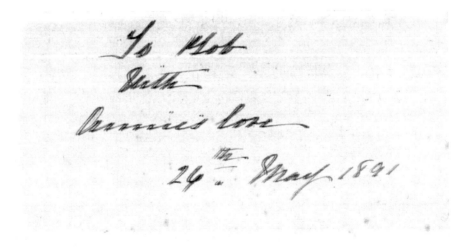

This inscription was written on the inside cover of our copy of "Views & Reminiscences"

Available soon...

A new edition of popular Inverclyde Folklore Book

It is the duty of every generation to preserve their folklore for the next, for in doing so we celebrate the past, present and future.

The remarkable tales of Inverclyde's past are brought to life in this beautifully illustrated and fascinating journey through the history of those times.

From ancient celtic sun worship to haunted country mansions, from the coast of Skelmorlie to the hills of Kilmacolm, pirates, sea serpents, saints and witches, these stories bring to light a rich seam of folk tradition, the forgotten history of Inverclyde.

This new edition features an extended appendices section and an introduction by Alisdair Gray

Magic Torch

175 Dalrymple Street, Greenock, Scotland, PA15 1JZ
email : magictorchgroup@hotmail.com